WINGS OF WAR

Training Planes of World War II

by Nancy Robinson Masters

Content Review:
Research Department
United States Air Force Museum

C A P S T O N E
H I G H / L O W   B O O K S
an imprint of Capstone Press

C A P S T O N E   P R E S S

818 North Willow Street • Mankato, Minnesota 56001
http://www.capstone-press.com

Printed in the United States of America.

Library of Congress Cataloging-in-Publication Data
Robinson Masters, Nancy.
  Training planes of World War II/by Nancy Robinson Masters.
    p. cm.--(Wings of war)
  Includes bibliographical references and index.
  Summary: Introduces the various kinds of World War II trainer planes, describes the missions for which they were used, and sketches the training required of their pilots.
  ISBN 1-56065-534-8
  1. Training planes--United States--History--Juvenile literature.
2. World War, 1939-1945--United States--Juvenile literature.
[1. Training planes. 2. Airplanes, Military. 3. World War, 1939-1945--Aerial operations.] I. Title. II. Title: Training Planes of World War Two. III. Title: Training Planes of World War 2. IV. Series: Wings of war (Mankato, Minn.)
UG1242.T67R63   1998
623.7'462'09709044--DC21

                                        97-6000
                                          CIP
                                          AC

The author would like to thank Harry Wadsworth, Laura Thaxton, and Bill Masters for their research assistance.

Editorial credits
Editor, Matt Doeden; cover design, Timothy Halldin; Illustrations, James Franklin; photo research, Michelle L. Norstad

Photo credits
American Airpower Heritage Museum, 15, 33, 35, 40
Archive Photos, 6, 9, 28, 47
Steve Butman, cover
Nancy Robinson Masters, 16, 20, 26
National Archives, 12, 23, 24, 36
Larry Sanders, 18, 31, 38
Lockheed Martin Skunk Works, 4

TABLE OF CONTENTS

Chapter One   Training for World War II 5

Chapter Two   Beginning Trainers 13

Chapter Three Later Trainers 17

Chapter Four   U.S. Flight Training 27

Chapter Five   World War II Trainers Today 37

Photo Diagram 40

Words to Know 42

To Learn More 44

Useful Addresses 45

Internet Sites 46

Index 48

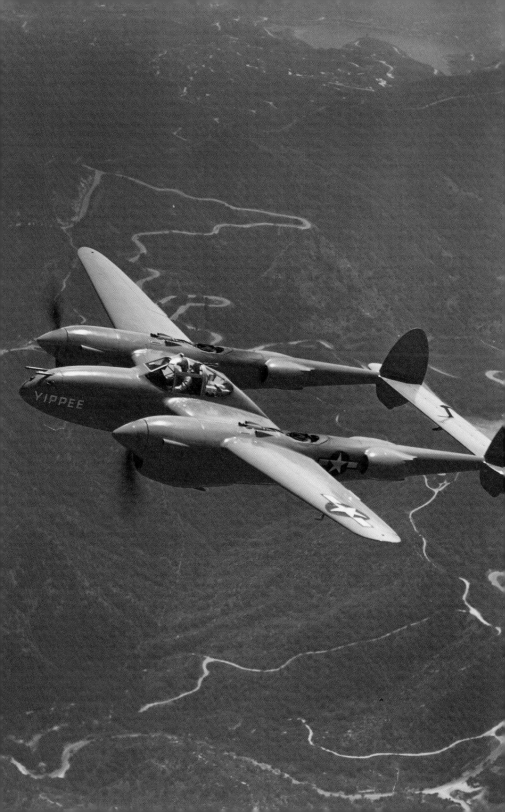

Training for World War II

Adolf Hitler used a large German military to attack Poland in 1939. One of Hitler's best weapons was a powerful air force. The German military's attack of Poland started World War II (1939-1945). The German, Japanese, and Italian militaries joined forces to form the Axis powers.

Great Britain, France, Canada, and Russia fought against the Axis powers. They were called the Allied nations. In 1941, the Japanese

The United States fought as one of the the Allied nations during World War II.

military bombed Pearl Harbor, Hawaii. The United States had a navy base at Pearl Harbor. The United States joined the Allies after the bombing.

World War II ended when the United States dropped two atomic bombs on Japan in 1945. An atomic bomb is a powerful explosive that destroys large areas. An atomic bomb leaves behind harmful elements after it explodes.

Preparing an Air Force

The United States did not wait until 1941 to prepare for World War II. Many U.S. leaders believed the United States would need a strong air force. The air force was part of the U.S. Army during World War II. It was called the U.S. Army Air Forces (AAF).

The AAF began training pilots, navigators, and bombardiers for war. Navigators map courses for pilots to fly. Bombardiers control where and when bombs are dropped from airplanes.

The U.S. military trained pilots for World War II.

Training Pilots

The U.S. military tested candidates who wanted to be pilots. A candidate was someone who was trying to become a pilot. Doctors made sure candidates were healthy. Candidates took intelligence tests. They took tests that measured their reaction times. Reaction time measures how quickly a person acts in a situation.

Candidates who passed the tests entered the AAF as cadets. A cadet is a military student. Most World War II cadets were young men. About eight out of 10 cadets had never been in an airplane before their training.

Cadets attended five levels of flight schools before they were ready for combat. They learned how to fly many kinds of airplanes. They learned to fly using instruments. They also learned how to use different airplanes' weapons.

Cadets attended flight schools before they were ready for combat.

UP AND AT'EM BOYS
KEEP 'EM' FLYING
AFTERNOON WING
DATE
FIRST PERIOD
SECOND PERIOD
THIRD PERIOD
FOURTH PERIOD
INSTRUCTOR STUDENT
Field #11-Down
Cadetwatch

Cadets flew more than 200 hours during their training. Some flew more than 350 hours. Cadets began by flying small airplanes. These airplanes had wooden frames covered with cotton cloth. They had one engine.

Cadets flew bigger airplanes as they became more experienced. They did not fly actual combat planes until they were almost finished with their training.

Effect on the War

Early in the war, Axis pilots were more experienced than Allied pilots. The experienced pilots gave the Axis powers an advantage over the Allies.

The Allies grew stronger by training pilots and building better airplanes. The trained Allied pilots could fly as well as the Axis pilots. The Axis powers no longer had an advantage.

MAJOR PACIFIC AIR BATTLES OF WORLD WAR II

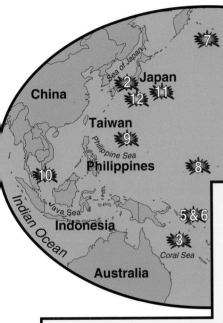

5. Guadalcanal Campaign,
   Aug., 1942 - Feb., 1943
6. Solomon Islands Campaign,
   Feb., 1943 - Nov.,1944
7. Battle of the Komandorski Islands,
   March 26, 1943
8. Truk Attack,
   Feb. 17-18, 1944
9. Battle of the Philippine Sea,
   June 19-20, 1944
10. Battle of Leyte Gulf,
    Oct. 23 - 26, 1944
11. Battle for Iwo Jima
    February, 1945
12. Atomic Bomb dropped on Hiroshima
    August 6, 1945

1. Pearl Harbor,
   Dec. 7,1941
2. Doolittle Raid
   April 18,1942
3. Battle of the Coral Sea,
   May 4-8, 1942
4. Battle of Midway,
   June 3-6, 1942

CHAPTER TWO

Beginning Trainers

Allied cadets learned to fly in small airplanes. Most of these airplanes were easy to fly. Many of them were tandem airplanes. Tandem means having two seats, one in front of the other. The cadet sat in the front seat. An instructor sat behind the cadet. Most Allied nations trained cadets in the same kinds of airplanes.

Stearman Kaydet

The first Stearman Kaydet flew in 1934. It was an open-cockpit airplane. A cockpit is the part of an airplane where the pilot sits. An open-cockpit

Allied cadets learned to fly in small airplanes.

airplane has no roof above the pilot's seat. The Kaydet helped pilots learn basic flying skills like how to use rudders. A rudder is the part of an airplane that causes it to turn.

The Kaydet flew at speeds up to 124 miles (199 kilometers) per hour. The Allies built more than 10,000 PT-13 Kaydets to train pilots for World War II. Most British cadets trained on Kaydets.

Fairchild Cornell

The Fairchild company built the first Cornell in 1938. The Cornell had two seats. Most Cornells had open cockpits, but some had canopies. A canopy is a cover above a cockpit.

The Fairchild Cornell flew at speeds up to 129 miles (207 kilometers) per hour. The Allies built more than 7,500 Cornells during World War II.

Stinson L-5 Sentinel

The Stinson L-5 Sentinel was not built as a training airplane. But the U.S. military used it to train pilots during and after World War II.

The Allies built more than 3,000 Sentinels during World War II.

The Sentinel was a sturdy airplane. It could withstand bumpy landings.

Some Sentinels had room for stretchers. The Allies used stretchers to carry wounded soldiers. British pilots carried supplies in some Sentinels. Sentinels could land at places larger airplanes could not.

Sentinels flew at speeds up to 100 miles (161 kilometers) per hour. The Allies built more than 3,000 Sentinels during World War II.

CHAPTER THREE

Later Trainers

Cadets flew bigger training airplanes with more instruments after they learned to fly small airplanes. Many cadets also practiced on machines called Link trainers.

Link Trainers

World War II Link trainers were the first flight simulators. A flight simulator is a machine that lets pilots practice flying while remaining on the ground. Link trainers looked like the cockpits of airplanes. Cadets handled the controls in Link trainers like airplane controls.

Link trainers looked like the cockpits of airplanes.

Cadets learned to fly large planes after they could fly small ones.

Cadets sat inside Link trainers. They could not see outside. They had to listen to instructors and follow instructions. This taught them to fly by using instruments instead of their eyes. Instruments in Link trainers measured things like speed, altitude, and gas. Altitude is the height of an object above the ground.

Most cadets spent 40 to 50 hours in Link trainers. About 500,000 pilots trained in these machines during World War II. Every country in the war used them for training, including the Axis powers.

Vultee Valiant

The Vultee BT-13 Valiant was the airplane most cadets flew during basic flight training. It was the first large airplane many cadets flew. It was heavier and harder to fly than smaller training airplanes.

The Valiant helped cadets learn to fly with control sticks. A control stick is the part of the airplane a pilot uses to steer.

Cadets called this airplane the Vultee Vibrator. This was because the Valiant's canopy shook and rattled whenever the aircraft dove or turned.

The Valiant was a tandem trainer. It flew at speeds up to 182 miles (293 kilometers) per hour. The Allies built more than 11,000 Valiants for World War II.

Bomber crews trained in the Beech AT-11 Kansan.

Beech AT-11 Kansan

Bomber crews trained in the Beech AT-11 Kansan during advanced flight school. A bomber crew included a pilot, a navigator, and a bombardier. The Kansan flew at speeds up to 215 miles (346 kilometers) per hour.

Bombardiers practiced bombing in the Kansan. They used 100-pound (45-kilogram) practice bombs. The practice bombs were bags filled with sand. Bombardiers released the practice bombs at targets. Instructors watched to see how close the bombardiers came to hitting the targets.

North American AT-6

The North American AT-6 was the most famous training airplane of World War II. Cadets who were training to be fighter pilots used the AT-6. The AT-6 was the last airplane many cadets flew with an instructor. The AAF called the AT-6 the Texan. The North American company built the AT-6 so it would handle like a fighter plane. The AT-6 helped prepare cadets to fly fighter planes.

The AT-6 flew at speeds up to 205 miles (330 kilometers) per hour. The Allies built more than 15,000 North American AT-6s for World War II. Every Allied nation gave the AT-6 a different name. The British called it the Harvard. Canadians called it the Yale. Australians called it the Wirraway.

AT-6 History

The Canadian military began flying an early model of the AT-6 in 1939. That year, Great Britain started sending cadets to Canada for training.

The United States was neutral in World War II until 1941. Neutral means not taking sides. The United States signed a Neutrality Act when the war began. Many U.S. leaders hoped the act would keep the United States out of the war. Under the Neutrality Act, U.S. pilots could not fly U.S.-built combat aircraft into Canada.

But the United States wanted the Allies to win the war. Canada and Great Britain needed U.S. planes. The AT-6 was one of the planes

The AT-6 was the most famous training airplane of World War II.

they needed most. American pilots flew AT-6s to the Canadian border. Then soldiers pushed them across the border into Canada. The Allies received the planes, but the U.S. did not break its agreement. A Canadian manufacturer began building the AT-6 in 1941.

Female Pilots and the AT-6

The Women's Airforce Service Pilots (WASPs) flew AT-6s. The WASPs were American women who volunteered to fly as ferry pilots. Ferry pilots flew airplanes from one military base to another. They helped make sure that each base always had enough airplanes. The U.S. military did not allow women to fly in combat.

WASPs had another job. They helped train cadets. WASPs pulled targets behind AT-6s. Fighter pilots practiced shooting the targets. They used real bullets. The bullets often hit the AT-6s. But the AT-6s were sturdy. AT-6 pilots were rarely hurt.

WASPs also helped the military test airplanes that had been repaired. They flew almost every model of airplane built during World War II.

The Women's Airforce Service Pilots flew AT-6 Texans.

CHAPTER FOUR

U.S. Flight Training

World War II cadets attended five levels of flight school before they were ready for battle. They began in ground school. Then they attended primary flight school, basic flight school, and advanced flight school. The last part of training was called the transition phase.

Ground School

Cadets trained to be soldiers at ground school. They exercised and attended classes. They studied subjects like math and science. They

World War II cadets attended five levels of flight school.

Cadets trained to be soldiers at ground school.

also learned about the codes pilots use to send messages when flying.

Ground school was also called pre-flight training. The AAF picked cadets for different jobs during ground school. The AAF chose navigators, bombardiers, and pilots. Each kind of cadet attended different schools after ground school.

Future navigators went to schools where they learned about guiding planes to exact locations. These cadets learned how to use maps. They learned to recognize landmarks like rivers and cities from the air.

Future bombardiers trained by dropping practice bombs from airplanes. Cadets dropped bombs from different altitudes. They also practiced dropping bombs in different weather conditions.

Future pilots went to primary flight school after ground school. There, they took their first flights.

Primary Flight School

Future pilots began flying at primary flight school. First they received about eight hours of instruction. Cadets who could not pass tests after this instruction were not allowed to fly.

Cadets spent ten weeks in primary flight school. They had 70 hours of flying time in small airplanes with light engines. The AAF used airplanes like the Stearman Kaydet and the Fairchild Cornell in primary flight school.

Some cadets trained at civilian schools during primary flight school. A civilian is a person who is not in the military. Civilians own and manage civilian flight schools. These flight schools trained cadets to fly small airplanes.

Basic Flight School

Cadets spent ten weeks at basic flight school. They learned to fly faster, heavier airplanes. Airplanes used in basic flight school were larger than those used in primary flight school. They also had more powerful engines.

Cadets had 70 hours of flying time during basic flight school. They learned how to fly in formations and how to fly at night. A formation is a group of airplanes flying together in a pattern.

The AAF used the Vultee Valiant to train cadets in basic flight school. Cadets also trained on Link trainers.

Some cadets trained in AT-6s during advanced flight school.

Advanced Flight School

Cadets went to advanced flight school after they proved they could fly the Valiant. Future fighter pilots attended single-engine advanced flight training. Future bomber pilots went to twin-engine advanced flight training. Advanced flight training lasted nine weeks.

Most bomber cadets trained in the Beech AT-11 Kansan. All cadets trained in the North American AT-6.

Cadets received silver wings when they completed advanced flight school. The silver wings meant they were AAF pilots. Pilots then entered the transition phase. The transition phase was the final training school.

Bomber Transition Phase

Pilots chosen to fly bombers entered the bomber transition phase. They learned to fly the airplanes they would use in battle.

Bomber pilots learned everything about their airplanes and weapons. They learned about the lands they would fly over. They learned about the ways enemies might attack.

Pilots flew different kinds of bombers. Many flew light and medium bombers. Others flew heavy bombers. Some flew Boeing B-29 Superfortresses. The B-29 was a very heavy bomber. It was the biggest airplane used in

Some cadets learned to fly the B-29 Superfortress.

World War II. The B-29 carried up to 20,000 pounds (9,072 kilograms) of bombs.

Pilots chosen to fly light, medium, and heavy bombers spent 10 weeks in the transition phase. They had 105 more hours of flying time. These pilots trained to fly bombers like the B-24 Liberator and the B-25 Mitchell.

Pilots chosen to fly the B-29 Superfortress had at least 300 hours of flying time. B-29 pilots spent about 16 weeks in the transition phase. They needed more time to learn how to fly their airplanes than other pilots.

Bomber pilots joined navigators and bombardiers during the transition phase. They formed bomber crews.

Fighter Transition Phase

Pilots selected to fly fighters spent five weeks in the transition phase. They spent 10 hours in the Bell P-39 Airacobra or the Curtiss P-40 Warhawk. Some pilots also trained on the Lockheed P-38 Lightning.

Fighter pilots practiced shooting machine guns at targets in the air. They practiced firing cannons and rockets at targets on the ground.

Fighter cadets trained in fighters like the P-39 Airacobra.

CHAPTER FIVE

World War II Trainers Today

The U.S. military had a surplus of trainers after World War II. Surplus means more than is needed. The military sent many surplus airplanes to airplane graveyards. An airplane graveyard is a place for old and unused planes.

Some trainers remained in service. The AT-6 Texan flew in the Korean War (1950-1953). The military sold other AT-6s to civilians. Civilians used them for jobs like

The military sent many surplus airplanes to airplane graveyards after the war.

Some World War II airplanes are still flying.

crop dusting. Crop dusting is spraying
chemicals on crops to keep insects away.

Still Flying
Some World War II airplanes are still flying.
Museums and collectors restore them. Restore
means to bring back to original condition.

Collectors display World War II airplanes at air shows. Air shows feature both old and new planes. People can see and touch the airplanes. The AT-6 is one of the most popular World War II planes at air shows. Some collectors sell rides in AT-6s.

Museums

Most World War II airplanes cannot fly anymore. Some of them are in museums.

The United States Air Force Museum near Dayton, Ohio, has many World War II airplanes. It has trainers like the AT-6 Texan and the Stearman Kaydet.

The National Air and Space Museum in Washington, D.C., has World War II airplanes. Museums give visitors a chance to learn about important parts of world history.

tail

wing

ROYAL NAVY
FK810

N60534

fuselage

tailwheel

AT-19 training plane

cockpit

nose

landing gear

WORDS TO KNOW

altitude (AL-ti-tood)—the height of an object above the ground

atomic bomb (uh-TOM-ik BOM)—a powerful explosive that destroys large areas; it leaves behind harmful elements after it explodes.

bombardier (bom-buh-DIHR)—a bombing crew member who controls where and when bombs drop from airplanes

cadet (kuh-DET)—a military student

canopy (KAN-uh-pee)—a cover over a cockpit

civilian (si-VIL-yuhn)—a person who is not in the military

combat (KOM-bat)—fighting between militaries

control stick (kuhn-TROHL STIK)—the part of an airplane a pilot uses to steer

crop dusting (KROP DUHST-ing)—spraying chemicals on crops to keep insects away

ferry pilot (FER-ee PYE-luht)—a pilot who flies airplanes from one military base to another

flight simulator (FLITE SIM-yuh-lay-tur)—a machine that lets pilots practice flying while remaining on the ground

formation (for-MAY-shuhn)—a group of airplanes flying together in a pattern

navigator (NAV-uh-gay-tuhr)—a bombing crew member who maps a course for the pilot to fly

neutral (NOO-truhl)—not taking sides

reaction time (ree-AK-shuhn TIME)—a measure of how fast a person acts in a situation

rudder (RUHD-ur)—the part of an airplane that causes it to turn

tandem (TAN-duhm)—having two seats, one behind the other

TO LEARN MORE

Asimov, Isaac. *How do Airplanes Fly?* Milwaukee: Gareth Stevens, 1993.

Baines, Francesca. *Planes*. New York: Franklin Watts, 1995.

Bowden, Joan Chase. *Planes of the Aces*. New York: Delacorte Press, 1993.

Masters, Nancy Robinson. *Airplanes of World War II*. Mankato, Minnesota: Capstone High/Low Books, 1998.

USEFUL ADDRESSES

American Airpower Heritage Museum
P. O. Box 62000
Midland, Texas 79711

National Air and Space Museum
Seventh Street and Independence Avenue
Washington, DC 20560

National Aviation Museum
P.O. Box 9724
Ottawa, Ontario KIG 543
Canada

United States Air Force Museum
Wright-Patterson Air Force Base
Dayton, OH 45433

INTERNET SITES

Military Aircraft Database
http://www.csd.uwo.ca/~pettypi/elevon/
   gustin_military/

Welcome To The National Warplane Museum
http://www.warplane.org

Stearman PT-13D "Kaydet"
http://www.wpafb.af.mil/museum/early_years/
   ey16.htm

WASP
http://www.infinet.com/~iwasm/wasp.htm

INDEX

Airacobra, 34
airplane graveyard, 37
Allied nations, 5, 13
altitude, 18, 29
AT-6, 21-23, 25, 32, 37, 39
atomic bomb, 7
Axis powers, 5, 10, 19

B-29, 32, 33, 34
bombardier, 7, 20, 21, 28, 29, 34

canopy, 14, 19
civilian, 30, 37
Cornell, 14, 30

ferry pilots, 25
formation, 30

ground school, 27-29

Hitler, Adolf, 5

Kansan, 20-21, 32
Kaydet, 13-14, 30, 39
Korean War, 37

Lightning, 34
Link trainers, 17-19, 30

museum, 38, 39

navigator, 7, 20, 28, 29, 34

Pearl Harbor, 7

Sentinel, 14-15
simulator, 17
surplus, 37

Valiant, 19, 31

Warhawk, 34

WASPs, 25